D1466241

Irish Prehistory
An Introduction

Anna Brindley

Country House, Dublin
in association with
The National Museum of Ireland

Published in 1994 by
Town House and Country House
Trinity House
Charleston Road
Ranelagh, Dublin 6
Ireland

in association with The National Museum of Ireland

British Library Cataloguing in Publication Data. A catalogue record for this book is available from the British Library.

ISBN: 0-946172-38-2

Acknowledgements
The author and publishers would like to thank the following for permission to reproduce their photographs: Dr B Raftery (Plate 6); Dr W O'Brien (Plate 8); Office of Public Works (Plates 1, 3); Liam Blake (Plate 11). Plate 9 is copyright of the author. All of the remaining photographs are the property of the National Museum of Ireland.

The author acknowledges the help of Professor Peter Woodman, J Jennings, D Whooley and J N Lanting. She is also grateful to the Biologisch-Archeologisch Instituut, Groningen, Netherlands, for the use of their research facilities during the preparation of the text.

Cover: Stone beads and pendants from Carrowkeel cemetery

Design and artwork: Bill and Tina Murphy
Colour origination: The Kulor Centre
Printed in Ireland by ßetaprint

CONTENTS

'Prehistory' refers to the time before writing was adopted, and is conventionally divided into a Stone Age, a Bronze Age and an Iron Age on the basis of the material used for weapons and tools. These periods are usually subdivided according to technological advances and cultural changes. In the absence of documentary evidence, the study of prehistory is based on material remains, be they tools, weapons, food remains, bones, seeds or even pollen. This book is an introduction to the Stone and Bronze Ages of Ireland.

THE PALAEOLITHIC OR OLD STONE AGE

The island of Ireland, lying on the westernmost margin of Europe, was formed slowly. Over countless millions of years, under the influence of massive volcanic and earthmoving forces, it was moulded into its present shape by alternating periods of intense heat and cold. The great cold spells, lasting tens of thousands of years, known as glaciations or Ice Ages, were broken by warmer spells (interglacials). During these warmer periods, trees, vegetation and warmth-loving animals spread northwards, and some cold-loving animals became extinct.

During the last Ice Ages, when much of Ireland was covered by massive layers of ice, the first humans began to colonise Europe. These people lived in caves, used stone tools and weapons, and hunted bison, mammoths and other now long-extinct animals. This early period of prehistory is known as the Old Stone Age or Palaeolithic, from Greek words meaning 'old stone'. Certain areas of Munster remained free of ice during at least part of the last Ice Age, so it is possible that some of the European colonists visited Ireland, but no evidence comparable to that found on the Palaeolithic settlements of Britain and mainland Europe has so far been discovered.

THE MESOLITHIC OR MIDDLE STONE AGE

Photo 1. Giant deer, standing 9 to 10 feet (3–3.5m) to the tips of their massive antlers, roamed the grassy plains of Ireland. Their huge antlers prevented them from living in forests, and when rising temperatures encouraged the spread of woodland, they became extinct.

In Ireland, from about 12000 BC onwards, temperatures rose to bring about an end to the last glaciation. A woodland vegetation gradually developed, which provided a home for the wildlife making its way from mainland Europe. Hares, stoats, pinemartens, otters and red deer, wolves, bears, wild pig and wild cat slowly colonised the developing landscape. The Irish giant deer, whose huge antlers prevented them from living in forests, soon became extinct (Photo 1). In the mixed woodland, hazel thickets, brambles and crabapple trees grew. Salmon and eel made their way up the rivers and streams, while on the still waters of the inland lakes, lilies produced edible seeds in profusion. With these colonists came men, women and children.

The earliest traces of people in Ireland date to about 7500 BC. By this time, the Irish climate was warmer and drier than it is today. These early settlers lived by collecting, fishing and hunting, exploiting the natural resources of woodland, river, lake and sea for all their needs. Their tools were made of stone, wood and bone, and their clothes of animal skins. An important piece of equipment, string, provided the basis for nets, baskets and traps, and the means with which items could be tied or bound together. Although the technology was simple, very fine craftsmanship was involved in making the tiny blades and points (microliths) of their composite tools and weapons (Photo 2). Scrapers and various types of axe were also used (Photo 3).

People whose existence is based on collecting and hunting are dependent on naturally occurring food sources and must move constantly, both to take

Photo 2. Mesolithic flint blades from Boora, Co Offaly. Several small blades like these, each about an inch (3cm) long, were placed lengthwise in a wooden handle and tied or gummed into place to make knives and harpoons.

advantage of seasonal abundances and in order not to exhaust local resources. Fish, hazelnuts, waterlily seeds and wild fruit were exploited on a seasonal basis. Riverside camps were used when trapping fish during the immensely important salmon and eel runs of the summer. Lake-edge camps were set up to take advantage of migrating water fowl in spring and autumn. Such dependence on seasonal resources would have limited the

Photo 3. Early Mesolithic axehead from Boora, Co Offaly, made of split mudstone (notice the flat but rough front surface) with neatly ground-down sides and end, and carefully sharpened blade.

number of people who could live together to small groups, probably family units, and necessitated a fairly isolated but highly mobile way of life.

By 4500 BC a change had taken place in stoneworking traditions. Ground mudstone axes had become more common, and composite tools made of microliths had been replaced by larger flakes of flint (known as 'Bann flakes'), (Photos 4, 5).

Photo 4. Single-piece weapons and tools made their appearance about 4500 BC. This simple knife was made by wrapping moss around the end of a Bann flake, which in turn was bound with twine or string. The imprint of the twine can still be seen on the moss. Found in the River Bann.

Photo 5. Bann flakes could also be used for spears and other weapons. In this reconstruction, three flakes form a three-pronged spear suitable for catching eels.

THE NEOLITHIC OR NEW STONE AGE

The word 'Neolithic' comes from the Greek words for 'new stone', and originally it denoted the period when polished stone tools were first used. It also refers to the prehistoric period when farming was first adopted.

The domestication of animals and the cultivation of plants started in southwest Asia and north Africa around 9000 BC. Farming, together with permanent settlements, pottery-making skills and the new tools needed for harvesting and processing grain, slowly spread across Europe, reaching Ireland some five thousand years later. By 3700 BC, hunting and gathering had largely been replaced by farming. This had a lasting impact on the Irish landscape. Open spaces had to be cleared and maintained for cultivation, and permanent settlements established. Cattle, sheep and goats, and wheat and barley, not native to Ireland, had to be imported. Cemeteries were used for the first time.

Neolithic settlements

The earliest farmers lived as family units in rectangular houses and practised mixed farming. Early permanent settlements were adapted to the mild but moist Atlantic-influenced climate. Unlike the houses of their European counterparts, which were sufficiently large to accommodate the animals during the winter months, Irish Neolithic houses were much smaller, as the climate was mild enough to allow the animals to remain outside all year round. The walls of the houses were constructed of split oak timbers set in trenches and held in position with small stones. Although permanent in that they were lived in all the year round, individual houses were used for a short period only, perhaps for a single generation. Wheat, some barley, sloes, blackberries, crabapples and hazelnuts have been found in these houses, as well as the bones of cattle, sheep, goats and pigs. Domesticated animals provided skins and hides for many purposes, bone for making tools, and a secure and predictable source of food, but there is no evidence for the use of dairy products or wool until later in the Neolithic period, or possibly in the Bronze Age.

Early household goods consisted of various containers, either woven

(Photo 6) or of pottery, which were used for storage and cooking, and small stone tools such as blades, knives and scrapers. Quernstones (Photo 7) were

Photo 6. Wooden containers, leather bags and woven baskets rarely survive. This handled basket from the Neolithic period, found in a bog at Twyford, Co Westmeath, was made by coiling long slivers of wood and binding them together with grass-like material.

Photo 7. Quernstones were one of the most essential tools of the Neolithic farmer. Grain had to be ground before it could be cooked and eaten. The earliest examples consist of two stones, one with a shallow depression into which the grain was poured, and a smaller stone used for rubbing or crushing the grain to make flour.

used to grind wheat. Grain was grown in small fields, probably close to the settlement. The fields would have been cultivated using hoes, digging sticks and simple stone ards (ploughs) and the grain harvested using flint-bladed sickles. Cattle and pigs must have grazed in the light woodland, sheep and goats in abandoned cleared areas, and wild fruits and mushrooms were available for the picking on the margins of the forest. During the winter months, trapping of small, thickly furred animals provided soft and warm material for clothing, while in the spring, netting of migrating geese and other birds would have supplied the larder before the crops were sown and while the domesticated animals were having their young.

Tools and weapons
Polished stone axeheads are almost invariably associated with farming. The large numbers found all over the country bear witness to the extensive woodland clearance that began to take place (Photo 8). Together with

chisels and adzes, they form the most characteristic polished tools of the Neolithic period. Any hard stone could be used to make them, but sometimes a particularly suitable stone was quarried and exchanged over long distances. Rough-outs were shaped by chipping, flaking or pecking, and then ground and polished on a grinding stone of sandstone (Photos 9, 10).

The recovery of numerous arrow-, lance- and javelin-heads (Photo 11) indicates the importance of hunting, either to protect animals and crops from predators or to supplement food stores. These weapons were also used in warfare.

Photo 8. Although stone axeheads from the Neolithic period have been found all over the country, their handles only survive in certain conditions, such as in bogs or rivers, where wood does not always decay. This axe and handle were found at Maguire's Bridge in Co Fermanagh.

Photo 9. Two rough-outs from Rathlin Island, Co Antrim, showing the early stages in the making of an axe. The example on the right has been flaked into shape and is ready for the time-consuming stage of grinding and polishing. The example on the left has been partially polished.

Photo 10. An axe-maker's stock. This well-used grinding stone and a group of finished axeheads were found together at Culbane, Co Derry.

Photo 11. Small stone tools were made using the same techniques as those employed for the making of axes. A suitably shaped piece of stone was procured, the edges were chipped to give either a sharp cutting edge or a blunt holding edge, and the flat sides were polished down to give a smooth surface. This lancehead found at Kilbeelaun, Co Galway, has chipped edges and smoothly polished flat surfaces.

Burial practices

Cemeteries are a feature of settled communities. During the Neolithic period, different rites were followed by individual groups at various times. Large stone tombs (megalithic tombs) were most popular in the northern half of the country and were used not only for burial, but probably also for other ceremonies. The most common types of megalithic tomb are the portal tomb, the court tomb and the passage tomb (Pl 1). In the southern half of the country, the earliest burials were much simpler, the body being placed in a pit with one or two small offerings. Later, two or three individuals were often buried together in small stone chambers, which were sealed up in large mounds and could not be opened again (Linkardstown-type burials). Sometimes offerings were left with the dead, such as pots (Photos 12, 12a), pieces of broken axes, and occasionally objects such as bone pins and beads (Pl 2).

Photos 12, 12a. The earliest pottery made in Ireland was round-based. This highly decorated pot was found in a Linkardstown-type burial at Baunogenasraid, Co Carlow. The decoration was carefully grooved into the damp clay before firing, probably in an open fire. (a) The base of the pot.

2

12a

Religion and symbolism

An important feature of fixed settlement is that complex religious and symbolic behaviour can be expressed in a permanent manner and rituals involving specially made vessels, tools and ornaments can evolve. During the Neolithic period, passage tombs were used for complex rituals which are not yet fully understood (Pl 3). The stones that line the passages and edge the mounds were sometimes decorated with abstract patterns. Stone was carefully worked to make large basins, smaller vessels (Photo 13) and items for unknown but probably ritual uses. Attractive coloured stone was traded for making beads of various shapes (Pl 4). Beautifully finished round balls like marbles were fashioned, and bone pins with carved shafts and heads were also used. Stoneworking sometimes reached a very high standard, as in the perforated maceheads made of specially chosen stone (Pl 5). The techniques employed were the same as those used to make axeheads, but the care taken in selecting the raw material, finishing off the articles, and the addition of time-consuming decoration, bear witness to the importance now given to ritual symbolism.

During the later stages of the Neolithic period, large earthen-banked enclosures and impressive circular wooden structures were built. These appear to have had a purely ceremonial function. New forms of flint arrowhead and of pottery were adopted. The pottery is distinguished by its flat bases (the earliest flat-based Irish pottery) and the grooved or cord-impressed decoration.

Transport and communications

In the heavily wooded environment of early Ireland, communication could most easily be effected along river margins or across comparatively lightly wooded higher ground. Clearance of the forest cover for agriculture encouraged the development of communications, as did the establishment of permanent settlements. Before the wheel was invented, items could only be transported on the backs of man and ox, or by boat. Ancient boats were made of animal or vegetable materials, and only survive in special conditions. The largest known Irish boat, all of 52 feet (16m) long, is also one of the oldest. It was found in a bog at Lurgan in Co Galway and was

made at the beginning of the Bronze Age. Logboats were made by hollowing out a straight tree trunk using an adze and sometimes fire, and could be of any size. The manufacture of logboats probably started in Ireland and Britain at the beginning of the Neolithic period. Before this, skin-covered boats must have been used both on the open sea and on inland waters. Sophisticated plank-built boats are known from the Middle Bronze Age in Britain, and were probably used here too. Logboats are found in bogs and lakes.

Photo 13. The patterns on this Neolithic stone urn were carefully pecked out and the smooth surfaces ground down where necessary using the same techniques as the artists employed to decorate the stones of the passage tombs.

The establishment of fixed paths and tracks through woodland and across the extensive bogs of Ireland was important to the development of communications and trade. The first primitive routeways must have been laid in relation to fixed natural points (high ground, rock outcrops, river crossings) and, when they became established, monuments and settlements. Such routeways would have been maintained chiefly by regular use. From an early stage, however, surfaced tracks were laid across bogs and moors. These took a variety of forms, including casual brushwood, hurdles, single beams laid end-to-end, and composite tracks of sleepers and runners. As the peat continued to grow, the tracks became incorporated in the bog and were preserved (Pl 6). The adoption of wheeled transport required wider and stronger tracks capable of bearing the weight of animals and carts and the wear of hooves and wheels (Photo 14).

THE EARLY BRONZE AGE

The term 'Bronze Age' signifies the change from a stone-based technology to one based on metal. The Bronze Age is conventionally divided into distinct periods, marked by growing sophistication in the use of metal. Pure copper was replaced in due course by bronze, which is an alloy of copper and tin and is harder and more durable (Pl 7). It would be wrong to imagine that each period was completely cut off from the next. Rather, the Bronze Age should be viewed as a time of continually evolving traditions.

Metallurgy and Beaker pottery

Around 2500 BC, metal started to replace stone as the basic material used eventually in the manufacture of almost all tools and implements. Ultimately, this change had enormous repercussions on every aspect of life. Metalworking required new sources of raw material, but also a revolutionary technology. The products, initially simple, were cheap and effective. The earliest items were made from the most malleable metals, pure soft copper, which could be cast easily and hammered to harden it, and gold, which could simply be beaten into sheets.

Soon the desire for metal led to mining — one mine in Killarney, County Kerry, dates to at least 2400 BC, and another at Mount Gabriel, County Cork, dates to 1700 BC (Pl 8). Ores were removed using a technique known as 'firesetting', a primitive but effective technique still used in parts of the world. This involved heating an area of rockface and dousing it with cold water. The shattered rock could then be knocked out. Torches of resinous pine chips lit the dark and wet mines while the ores were dislodged with stone hammers and wedges, before being carried to the surface in baskets. Here it was crushed and smelted in primitive furnesses to produce ingots (metal bars). By this means, large quantities of copper were obtained.

Just as the earliest farmers may be distinguished by the types of tool and container they used, early metal users may be recognised by their distinctive pottery, burial practices and rituals, as well as their tools. They used a particular type of pottery called 'Beaker' pottery, which was made and used

Photo 15. This arrowhead from Gortrea, Co Galway, shows the distinct barbs that characterised these weapons of the Early Bronze Age and, still preserved, the gut binding around the tang, which originally held it to the shaft. Wooden shafts and gut binding are occasionally found in bogs.

all over Europe, where metalworking was introduced at this time. Beaker pottery was often decorated with horizontal lines or geometric patterns, incised or made by impressing a square-toothed comb, cord, shell or fingernail.

Stone was still used for many small and commonplace tools, as well as for the new but characteristic archer's equipment of small barbed-and-tanged arrowheads (Photo 15) and wrist-guards. Bows of flexible yew are occasionally found preserved in bogs. The earliest copper tools were very simple, flat, trapezoidal-shaped axeheads, tanged knives and awls (Photos 16, 17). Gold, which is too soft for toolmaking, was hammered into ornamental strips or discs (Photo 18).

Photo 16. A small hoard of Early Bronze Age tools from Knocknagur, Co Galway. The dagger, axeheads and awls are of pure copper. They were cast in simple one-piece moulds and hammered into their final shape. The awls were used in leather-working.

Cooking methods

One of the most widespread means of cooking food was to place it in leather or skin containers and cook it by adding heated stones. Used in this way, stone shatters quite quickly and must be discarded at short intervals. Food could also be roasted and baked using specially dug pits and hot stones. By the Early Bronze Age, this method had evolved considerably, although the basic technique remained the same. A wooden water-filled trough was brought to boiling point by adding hot stones. As they shattered in the cold water, the stones were removed and thrown to one side, where they accumulated over a period of time. The hot water, which could be maintained at boiling point quite easily, was then used for cooking, bathing or industrial purposes. The heaps of discarded fire-cracked stones, known as *fulachtaí fia*, are often found in wet lowlying areas, close to springs and streams, where the watertable would have allowed the trough to fill and remain full. The dwellings were probably located nearby, but on drier ground.

Certain types of pottery vessel could also be used for cooking directly over an open fire, and burnt food is quite often found on pottery used for this purpose.

Photo 17. Axes and daggers were sometimes decorated. This fine example of a bronze axehead in mint condition was found in a leather pouch at Brockagh, Co Kildare.

Photo 18. The elegant ornament on these two Early Bronze Age gold discs from Tedavnet, Co Monaghan, was made by pressing out the pattern from the back, a technique known as 'repoussé'. Despite the simplicity of the pattern and the techniques used, the quality of the craftsmanship is unmistakable.

Burial customs

Some of the early metallurgists built megalithic tombs, known as wedge tombs, for their dead (Pl 9). The use of communal ancestral megalithic graves gradually ceased around 2300 BC and was replaced by individual burial, which continued in one form or another for at least the next thousand years. The earliest burials were either in simple pits or in cists (stone-lined graves), and these graves occur both singly and in cemeteries. The cemeteries are usually quite small, with less than half a dozen graves, each very often containing the remains of more than one individual.

Over the centuries some changes were made in the funerary rites. Often the bodies were placed in a crouched position in the grave, at other times the dead were cremated and their burnt bones were buried. Sometimes a small, highly decorated pot (Photo 19), and very occasionally other

Photo 19. Early Bronze Age pottery is almost invariably highly ornamented, with complex geometric patterns often arranged in horizontal bands, sometimes even on the base. The decoration on the base of this bowl food vessel from Grange, Co Roscommon, was impressed using a small square-toothed comb.

cont. p 33

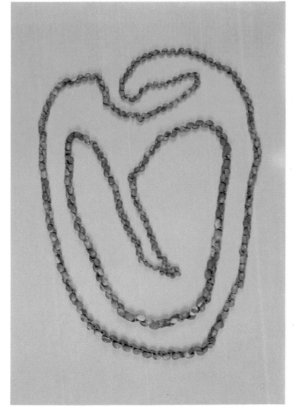

Pl 1. Megalithic tombs usually consist of a burial chamber surrounded by a mound of earth or stone, which is confined by a kerb of large stones. In this Neolithic passage tomb, the earthen mound has disappeared during the course of the last five and a half thousand years. Grave 7, Carrowmore, Co Sligo.

Pl 2. These necklaces, made from sea shells, date to the Neolithic period and are the oldest known Irish necklaces. Some of the shells have been pierced, while others have been rubbed against a stone and a cord threaded through the chamber of the shell. Found in the Phoenix Park, Dublin.

*Pl 3. (Facing page)
During the winter
solstice the sun shines
through a specially
constructed opening
above the entrance
to the Newgrange
passage tomb in
Co Meath, and
down the long
passage into the
chamber. The
technical
accomplishment is
clear, but the
purpose behind it is
not.*

*Pl 4. Beads,
pendants, buttons
and pins, often made
of bone, antler or
stone, are sometimes
found in Neolithic
tombs and burial
sites. These beads
were found in
passage tombs and
were probably
attached to the
clothing of the dead.*

*Pl 5. Elaborately
decorated stone
macehead from
Knowth, Co Meath.*

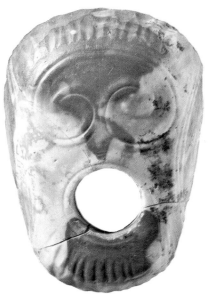

*Pl 6. This trackway,
which has been
dated to the Later
Bronze Age, was
discovered in a bog
at Garryduff,
Co Galway.*

*Pl 7. (Facing page)
An Early Bronze Age
copper 'cake' or ingot
and a flat copper
axe, found together
at Knockasarnet,
Co Kerry. The axe
was cast in a one-
piece mould.*

Pl 8. The curved roof of Mine 3 at Mount Gabriel, Co Cork, is due to the use of a technique known as 'firesetting', the chief means employed to remove rock containing copper ore. A wooden shovel, pick and torches were found in this mine.

Pl 9. Wedge tombs like this one at Parknabinnia, Co Clare, consist in their simplest form of two side walls, a wider and higher end (shown here), usually facing westwards, and a short end wall. These structures were often surrounded by several low walls and a cairn (mound of stones).

Pl 10. Food vessels and funerary urns of the Early Bronze Age. (Back row) Two encrusted urns, Ballyconnell, Co Wicklow and Agower, Calary Lower, Co Wicklow. (Middle row, from left) Bowl food vessel, Grange, Co Roscommon; three vase food vessels, Ballinchalla, Co Mayo, Stonepark, Co Mayo and Greenhills, Co Dublin. (Front) Pygmy cup from Greenhills, Co Dublin.

Pl 11. Stone circles seem to have played a role in celestial-related ceremonies in the later stages of the Early Bronze Age. Drombeg, Co Cork.

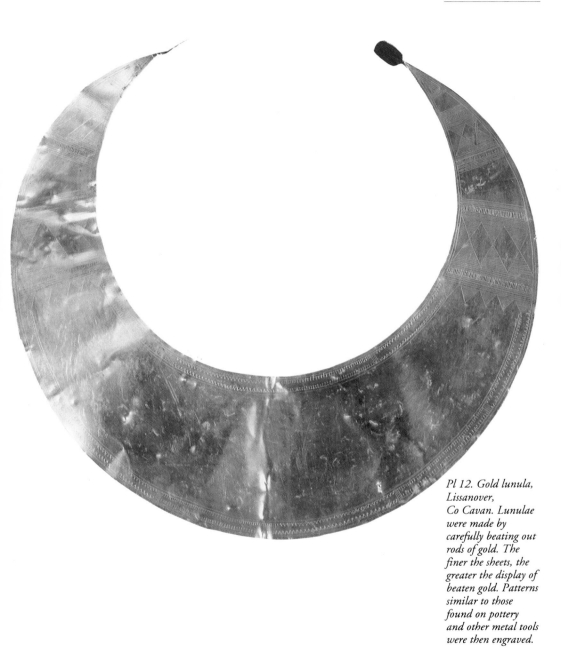

Pl 12. Gold lunula,
Lissanover,
Co Cavan. Lunulae
were made by
carefully beating out
rods of gold. The
finer the sheets, the
greater the display of
beaten gold. Patterns
similar to those
found on pottery
and other metal tools
were then engraved.

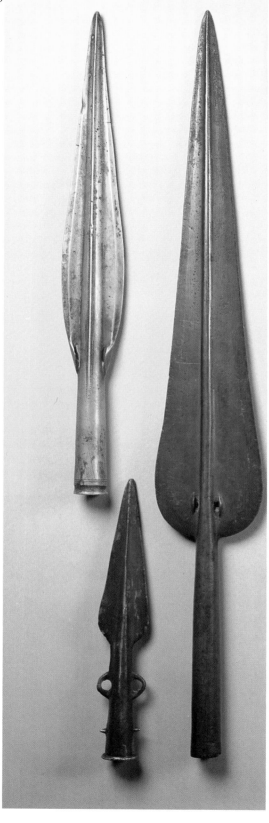

13

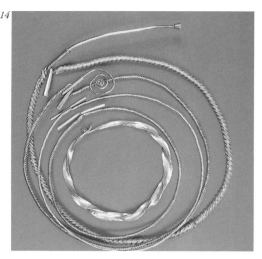

14

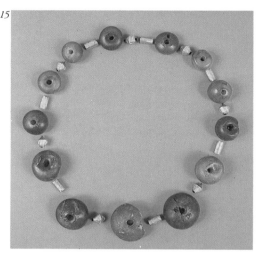

15

Pl 13. A selection of spears from the Later Bronze Age. (Top left) Decorated bronze spearhead of peghole type, from the River Shannon at Lanesborough, Co Longford. (Bottom left) Bronze spearhead with loops on socket. (Right) Bronze spearhead with loops in blade, found near Maghery, Co Monaghan.

Pl 14. Later Bronze Age gold ornaments known as 'torcs', made by twisting rods or ribbons of gold. The smaller torcs were neck ornaments, but it is not clear for what purpose the larger ones were used. The centre torc was found near Ballina, Co Mayo, while the two outer torcs are from Tara, Co Meath.

Pl 15. Amber and jet were also used to make neck ornaments. This necklace, from Cruttenclough, Co Kilkenny, consists of large beads of imported amber and smaller decorated conical and tubular beads of sheet-gold.

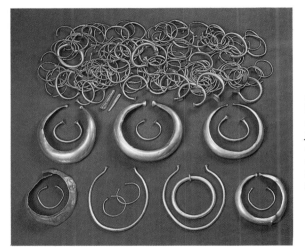

Pl 16. Part of an immense hoard of Later Bronze Age gold objects found in 1854 at Mooghaun, Co Clare, consisting of bracelets, neck ornaments and gold ingots.

Pl 17. This gorget from Glenisheen, Co Clare, consists of a crescent-shaped sheet with repoussé ornament and composite disc terminals, each having two separate ornamented discs joined by folding the edges together.

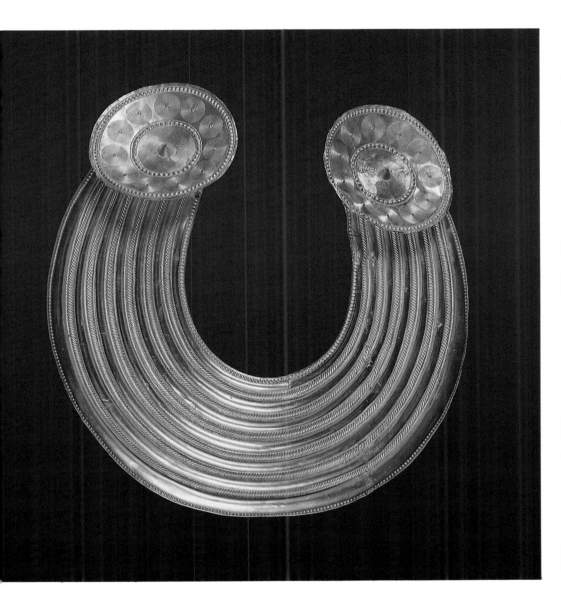

Pl 18. This Later Bronze Age hoard of jewellery found at Banagher, Co Offaly, probably belonged to a private individual who hid it and was unable to retrieve it later. The necklace has 125 beads of imported amber, two of the bracelets are of bronze, the penannular bracelet is gold, and the fourth item is a small gold dress-fastener.

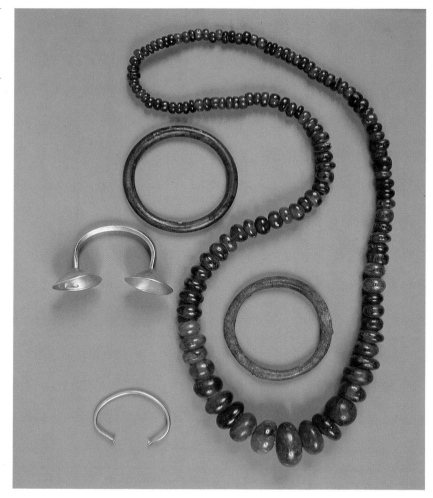

Pl 19. A large cauldron found in a bog at Castlederg, Co Tyrone. Cauldrons of this size were probably used for ceremonial purposes.

cont. from p 20

personal possessions, were left in the grave. These pots are called 'food vessels' because their shape suggests that they may have contained food or drink. When cremation became more popular, the bones were often placed in these vessels, or the food vessel was turned upside down beside the burnt bones. Later, very large pots or urns became popular for burial (Pl 10). These were usually highly ornate vessels which were turned upside down over the cremated bones to form a decorative cover. In some cases, food vessels and tiny incense cups were put in with the urn, and occasionally daggers, battle axes, pins and beads were included. By the Late Bronze Age, it had become fashionable to put the cremated bones in a large upright pot.

The cist graves were generally of two types, rectangular/subrectangular (Photo 20), or polygonal, where the side walls produced a more circular shape. Sometimes the floor was also paved. Cists were commonly

Photo 20. A rectangular cist in an Early Bronze Age cemetery at Keenoge, Co Dublin. The crouched position of the skeleton is typical of the period, as is the decorated food vessel in front of the head.

constructed by digging a pit and setting stones inside it. After burial had taken place and the capstone was positioned on top of the cist, the pit was filled in and sometimes covered with a mound of earth. Occasionally the grave was enclosed by a circular ditch. The rectangular cists were used for both inhumation and cremation burials. Polygonal cists, which were too small for inhumation (unburnt) burial, were used chiefly for cremated bones until close to the end of the Early Bronze Age, when simple unprotected pits became fashionable.

Ritual, symbolism and ornaments

Prehistoric religious beliefs are difficult to recreate or even recognise today, but occasionally we gain a shadowy glimpse of them through the surviving material evidence. A large wooden idol found in a Cavan bog may have formed part of a temple or cult house (Photo 21). Similarly, we know that from the middle of the Neolithic period, there was a growing interest in and knowledge of the movements of the stars and the sun. This probably reflects the needs of farmers to predict sowing seasons and of seafarers to predict the position of the stars for navigation. Stone circles, rows of stones and single stones seem to have played a role in celestial-related ceremonies in the later stages of the Early Bronze Age, but the precise way in which these monuments were used is still a mystery (Pl 11).

Gold discs, possibly worn in pairs sewn onto clothes, and hair ornaments known rather confusingly as 'basket earrings' but now thought to have been held in the hair, were worn by the early metal users. The first truly spectacular ornaments are the lunulae (Pl 12). These are crescent-shaped collars of beaten gold with finely incised patterns (Photo 22). Lunulae are never found in burials, which suggests that they were regarded as family heirlooms or items of hereditary prestige and status, rather than personal property. Jet (a black, shiny, coal-like substance) was also used for multi-strand necklaces (Photo 23). Bone pins, simpler jet bead necklaces (Photo 24) and bronze bracelets are occasionally found in graves, which suggests that these were the property of individuals.

Photo 21. Wood must have been used for many purposes in the past, as it was readily available and easily carved, but it only survives in very dry or very wet conditions. This idol, from Ralaghan, Co Cavan, has been scientifically dated to the middle of the Bronze Age.

Photo 22. This lunula from Ross, Co Westmeath, worn by a model, shows the finely incised decoration that is characteristic of these ornaments.

Photo 23. Early Bronze Age jet necklace found at Cumber, Co Down. Jet had to be imported, so it was probably rarer and possibly more valuable than gold.

Photo 24. Simple jet bead necklace found in a grave at Keenoge, Co Dublin. Jet and amber were used to make small ornaments such as buttons and beads.

Developments in early metallurgy

By 1200 BC, over a thousand years had elapsed since metallurgy was first practised in Ireland, and considerable development had taken place during that period. Two-piece stone moulds (Photo 25) were often expertly carved and could be used to cast a variety of different tools. The moulds themselves are a useful indicator of the types of tool being made at any one

Photo 25. Two-piece stone moulds, one for a spearhead with loops on the socket, the other for a palstave axe, a type intermediary between a flat axe and a socketed axe.

time. The demand for better tools led to the abandonment of stone as a raw material for most tools and to the development of new types of metal tools, weapons and ornaments. Technical expertise also resulted in more efficient tools (Photo 26), while developments in casting techniques, from stone moulds, to core casting, to clay moulds in the Late Bronze Age, led to the invention of socketed tools.

Photo 26. Reconstructed handles for a flat axe (top), palstave axe (middle) and socketed axe (bottom). (The axeheads are originals.)

THE LATER BRONZE AGE

The later stages of the Bronze Age in Ireland are identified with a period of huge metal production, vast resources, strife, environmental change, and changes in ritual practices.

From about 1200 BC onwards, there are many indications that a change in environmental conditions was having a detrimental effect on practically every aspect of life. The impact of widescale woodland clearance and exploitation of soils had already led to the spread and accumulation of blanket-bog on high ground from the end of the Neolithic period. By the middle of the Bronze Age, significant waterlogging of lowlying areas was also beginning to occur. Agricultural land, the basis of all wealth in the days before trade, had previously been relatively plentiful. Now, it was sandwiched much more tightly between the spreading wet and ill-drained lowlying areas and the wet and cold uplands. The resulting pressure on land resources played an important role in the changes in society at this time. An increase in warfare, and a subsequent increase in the demand for arms, also acted as a stimulant to the bronze-based industries that now emerged.

900 BC marks the beginning of a period of great technological mastery. The addition of lead to bronze and the use of clay moulds led to the production of technically sophisticated cast products, such as horns. Improved techniques of sheet metalworking, riveting and soldering meant that large items such as buckets and cauldrons could now be manufactured. Immense quantities of weapons were made, and specialist and all-purpose tools such as chisels, gouges, punches, tweezers, sickles and knives were produced in large numbers, as were ornaments of gold, amber and jet.

Weapons

By the end of the Early Bronze Age, many individuals carried arms, such as knives, daggers, halberds (long-handled battle-axes), small flint arrowheads and, no doubt, axes. These were gradually replaced by purpose-designed weapons, such as rapiers, spears, swords and shields. Large numbers of these have been found, suggesting that personal protection was now considered necessary. Small daggers gradually increased in size as technical expertise developed, and were replaced eventually by long, sometimes very narrow, rapiers (Photo 27). Whereas knives and daggers have many uses other than stabbing, rapiers are really only suitable for thrusting and fencing — they are specialised weapons developed for face-to-face fighting. In the Late Bronze Age, swords with cast handles and wider, leaf-shaped blades replaced the long straight-sided rapiers (Photo 28). These swords were primarily slashing weapons, and may have been used by fighters mounted on horseback. Shields made of leather, wood and bronze were carried for protection (Photos 29, 29a). Spearheads of various types, and sometimes of impressive proportions, completed the array of weapons an individual might carry. Small kite- and leaf-shaped spearheads may have been used for hunting, while the larger examples were probably used for combat or display (Pl 13).

Photo 27. (Bottom left) Early Bronze Age dagger; (bottom right) Later Bronze Age socketed dagger; (middle left and right) Later Bronze Age swords; (centre) rapier of the middle stage of the Bronze Age.

Photo 28. (Facing page) As with axes, the handles of Later Bronze Age rapiers and swords were as important as the blade. (Top) rapier with well-preserved bone handle still riveted in place; (middle) sword still retaining part of a bone handle; (bottom) sword with cast handle and holes for rivets.

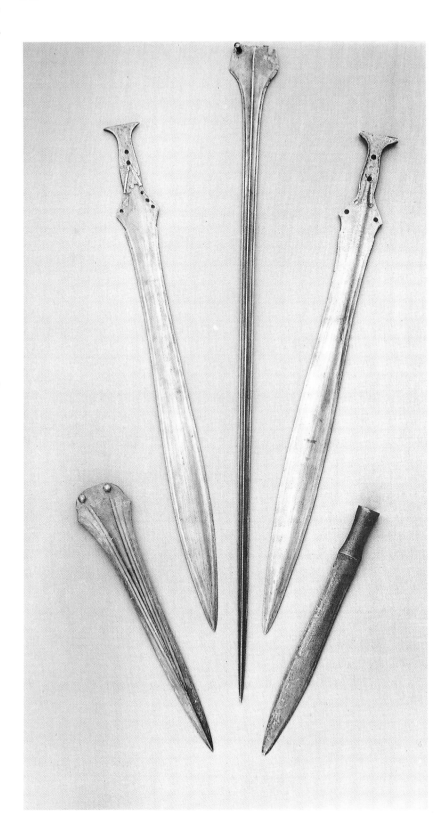

28.

29.

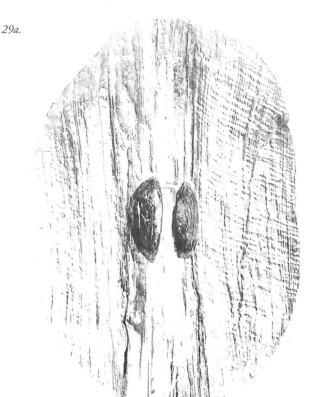

29a.

*Photo 29, 29a.
Later Bronze Age
carved, one-piece
wooden shield, with
large central boss
(stud) and
concentric raised
bands, found at
Annandale,
Co Leitrim. The boss
covers a carved
wooden handle at
the back (29a), but
the concentric bands
are purely
ornamental.*

Ornaments, insignia, prestige and wealth

Weapons were not only used in combat; they were also carried to intimidate and impress, for ceremonial purposes and individual prestige. During the later stages of the Bronze Age, these functions were also fulfilled by a wide range of ornaments and insignia. Considerable resources and technical expertise were employed to make ornaments of gold, amber, jet and bronze (Photo 30).

Photo 30. Simple and sophisticated techniques were used side by side to make fine ornaments. This necklace from Derrinboy, Co Offaly, was made by winding gold wire around a fine leather thong.

Bronze neck and arm ornaments and pins were cast and decorated with incised patterns, but the most spectacular ornaments were made of gold. Soft, malleable gold was cast, hammered, soldered and twisted to form magnificent ornaments, which were further enhanced by incised and repoussé work. Amber, which is found on the coasts of the Baltic Sea and is sometimes washed up on the coasts of Britain and the Netherlands, was imported and used in large quantities in necklaces, some of which comprised several hundred beads (Pls 14, 15, 16). The exhibition of wealth by wearing large amounts of gold in the form of huge collars (Pl 17), enormous dress-fasteners, lock-rings, hair ornaments and bracelets, suggests that certain individuals displayed their wealth at particular times, possibly during ceremonies.

Hoards and votive offerings

A feature of the Bronze Age, but especially its later stages, was the deposition of hoards and votive offerings. A hoard is a group of objects hidden for safe-keeping. Hoards of various types are known: founders' hoards (with scrap metal and ingots), merchants' hoards (new objects for trade) and personal hoards (private possessions) (Pl 18). Bronze Age hoards were usually hidden on dry land. The rise in the number of hoards deposited during this period suggests that the possibility of retrieving goods hidden for safe-keeping was limited.

Votive offerings are made with no intention of retrieval. Bronze Age votive offerings may consist of single objects, large numbers of objects deposited at one time, or repeated offerings at one place where they accumulated. A large proportion of all the weapons that have been found have been discovered in rivers, lakes or bogs that cover the sites of former lakes. Although it is impossible to ascertain why these offerings were made, the threat to livelihood posed by shrinking agricultural resources, caused by the growth of bogs, may have led to ceremonies involving the donation of offerings, especially weapons, but also other costly and valuable objects, to water gods and spirits.

Cauldrons

Cauldrons of wood or sheet bronze were made in increasing numbers from the twelfth century BC onwards, and were one of the most impressive products of the Late Bronze Age (Pl 19). The wooden examples were hand-carved, of poplar or alder. Food and liquids could have been cooked in them by continually adding hot stones. The bronze cauldrons were made of hammered sheets, with each cauldron comprising a number of sheets held together by hundreds of individually made rivets. Bronze cauldrons could be suspended over a fire or heated by adding hot stones to their contents. Fleshhooks (long-handled fork-like implements) were used for removing hot meat. Cauldrons were valued items and were probably used by the wealthy and powerful for ceremonial feasting.

Music

The oldest surviving musical instruments in Ireland are the cast bronze horns of the Late Bronze Age (Photo 31). However, horns, bone whistles and drums made of wood and skin were probably used for a long time before it became possible to cast large objects in metal. The Late Bronze Age horns are single-piece instruments of two types, side- and end-blow, and each produces a different sound when played in the manner of the Australian didgeridu. Side- and end-blow horns are often found together, suggesting that they were played together. They are the product of a most complex technology, involving unparalleled control over the casting processes, where the manufacture of very regular thin walls was essential to the finished product. Other cast items that were used for musical purposes include rattle-pendants (Photo 32) and crotals (rattles) (Photo 33). Crotals are grenade-shaped hollow objects containing a small pebble or similar item, and they may have been used as primitive bells.

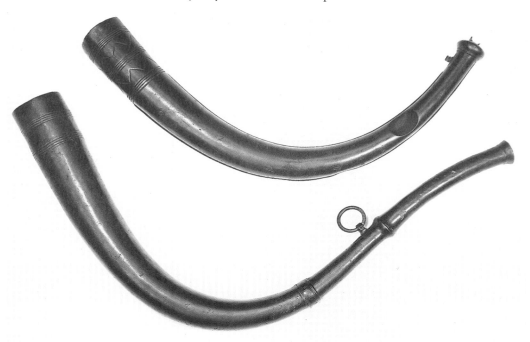

*Photo 32. Rattle-
pendants provided
an accompaniment
similar to the
modern playing of
spoons or castanets.
They may have been
attached to horse
harnesses, but they
could also have been
successors to hand-
held wooden and
bone examples.
Found at Lissanode,
Co Westmeath.*

*Photo 33. A crotal
with cast ornament.
The object may have
functioned as a
rattle used as a
musical
accompaniment, or
it may have had a
purely ritual
purpose.*

Settlements

A large number of settlements from the middle of the Bronze Age onwards
have been discovered. Groups of small circular houses, often enclosed by
banks, walls or palisades, or constructed on small islands, promontories or
lake edges, suggest local tensions and insecurity. At the same time, the
enclosure of settlements on remote and inhospitable mountaintops and
seabound promontories with earthen banks and ditches would seem to
indicate a banding together of communities against an outside threat.
Towards the end of the Late Bronze Age, some of these settlements had
become centres of power, both of a secular and a ritual nature.

The wet environments of the waterside settlements allowed for greater
preservation of wooden structures and artefacts compared to earlier periods.
Wooden bowls and platters and larger items such as cauldrons and shields
point to expert carpentry before lathe-turning was introduced. Some
woollen cloth and sophisticated horse-hair tassels (Photo 34) reflect
expertise in textile-making. A wide range of bronze socketed tools, both for
general purpose and specialist work, have survived, all made in clay moulds,
fragments of which are found on many sites. Coarsely made undecorated
pottery was used for cooking and storage, and also as containers for the
cremated bones of the dead (Photo 35).

Burial practices

The burials of the Late Bronze Age are remarkably undistinguished by either grave furnishings or offerings compared to those of the Early Bronze Age. The dead were invariably cremated and the bones placed in ordinary, rather unattractive, pots. These were buried in pits, which were sometimes surrounded by a small ditch or a low mound. In some graves there were no pots, but it is possible that containers of leather or other materials were used and have since decayed.

Photo 35. An example of Later Bronze Age pottery. This pot was found in a grave at Rathgall, Co Wicklow, and contained cremated bones.